# Contents

# 1

# Introduction

Nostalgia is defined as the affection for the past, but what makes the '90s so great, and why do we long to relive those days? For most who decided to pick up this book, it's because the '90s were a significant part of their childhood. Things are great when you are a kid because you don't have bills to pay, don't have major responsibilities, and have a ton of free time to hang out with friends and enjoy new experiences. But that's not the only reason the '90s was a fantastic decade.

We had incredible advancements in technology. We got to see the gaming industry blow up and were the first use to use early-generation gaming systems, from the Nintendo to the PlayStation. Our fashion consisted of bold neon colors, jelly shoes, and fanny packs. And our taste in music came in a variety of genres.

We loved to spend our Friday nights heading out to the local video store such as Blockbuster, and we loved to rent the "New Releases." During this time, they were brand new movies that had just recently left the theater. It still makes me mad that "New Releases" on Netflix are movies from 2015. It just does not translate with what Blockbuster taught me in the 90s!

Our world at that time was not overrun by technology. We didn't suffer from "tech-neck." You lived in a period when the internet, as we know it today, was in its infancy. We didn't have social media, and the # symbol was known as a pound symbol, not a hashtag! The '90s was a decade of growth and innovation across almost every industry. You could practically even refer to it as an experiment that led to a quantum leap in technology.

Think about the music industry; we went from using cassettes in the early '90s, then fully transitioning to CDs by the mid-'90s, then before the decade was over, we were already onto MP3s. Talk about a massive upgrade in a short period of time. The same holds true for the film industry. It almost felt like overnight, a shift happened where the video stores phased out VHS, and DVDs started to become mainstream. A lot of things were changing in this decade.

Additionally, it was a decade that was also a major stepping stone for telecom. First, we were introduced to the "car phone," but not many people had them unless they were "important enough" to have one. Then by the mid to late '90s, we all went through a Nokia craze. That was our first access to the original popular cellphone. Notice, I said cellphones, not smartphones, because the technology was not there just yet. But, back then, teenagers didn't really have cellphones, but we had beepers, and you weren't considered 'cool' unless you had one.

Overall it was a magical decade that I wish I could step back in time and experience. But, as our current world continues to advance in technology, it's likely not going to be all that far-fetched in the near future. We may be able to take a stroll back down memory lane with the help of the Metaverse.

# 2

# Television in the '90s

I f you grew up in the 1990s, chances are good that you remember having a massive television set in your living room. Let's take a stroll down memory lane and take a look at some of the defining TV technologies of the 90s.

These tube TVs were cumbersome, but they were the standard at the time. Today, of course, we have sleek flat-screen models that take up far less space and save a lot more energy. But how did we get from there to here?

Well, at the beginning of the decade, most of us had very large CRT screens. These are now known as vintage TV technology, but during the '90s, the demand started to grow for bigger screen TVs, and we started to transition. By the end of the decade, we started introducing plasma TVs, but they were costly at the time, so still, most homes did not have the newest TV technology.

Although since the '90s, technology has changed rapidly—and television is no different. Today's TVs are sleek, powerful machines that offer a viewing experience light years ahead of what was available in the 1990s. But even though the TVs of the '90s were nowhere near as technologically advanced as today's TVs, those old boxy CRTs will always have a special place in our hearts.

# 3

# Iconic TV Shows

I t's hard to believe that it's been more than 20 years since the '90s ended. That decade was a golden age for television, giving us some of the most iconic shows of all time. From "Full House" to "Friends" to "The Fresh Prince of Bel-Air," there were so many great programs to choose from. But what made '90s TV so special? Let's take a look back at why TV shows in the '90s were so great.

One of the best things about TV in the '90s was that there was truly something for everyone. Whether you were into comedies, dramas, sci-fi, or animation, there was a show that fit your taste. And unlike today, where most shows are aimed at a specific demographic, many '90s shows had crossover appeal. That meant that they could be enjoyed by people of all ages, which led to some truly timeless classics.

In recent years, there has been a lot of criticism of the quality of writing on television. While it's true that there are some shows with less-than-stellar writing, that was definitely not the case in the '90s. The vast majority of shows during that decade were extremely well-written, with clever plots and witty dialogue. Shows like "Seinfeld," "Friends," and "The Simpsons" set a high bar for writing that is still unmatched today.

I'm going to highlight a few favorites from this decade to help you get those nostalgic vibes.

## Home Improvement - Comedy - 1991 - 1999

Home Improvement was one of the most popular TV shows of the 1990s. The show starred Tim Taylor, a suburban father who was always trying (and usually failing) to do home improvement projects around his house. Even though Tim was accident-prone and often made things worse, viewers loved him because he was relatable. He was just a regular guy who was trying his best to take care of his family.

In addition to Tim, the show had several other characters that viewers came to love. There was Jill, Tim's wife, and their three boys; Al, Tim's friend and neighbor who owned an auto shop; and Wilson, the neighbor who always had sage advice for Tim but whose face was always obscured by the fence between their houses. Plus, if you were a teen fan girl, then you clearly had a crush on Johnathan Taylor Thomas and at least three posters of him pinned up to your bedroom walls!

The show always captured a lot of attention and even attracted other A-list celebrities as special guests on the show, from Jay Leno to Pamela Anderson.

Home Improvement was one of the most popular TV shows of the 1990s for a good reason – it was funny, family-friendly, and had a great cast. If you're looking for something to watch with your kids or something to remind you of simpler times, then you can't go wrong with Home Improvement.

**Law & Order - Crime - 1990 - 2010**

I'll admit it, I'm a bit of a television junkie, and one of my favorite shows from that era was Law & Order. One of the things that made Law & Order so great was its characters. Viewers got to know and love Detectives Lennie Briscoe (played by Jerry Orbach) and Ed Green (played by Jesse L. Martin), ADA Serena Southerlyn (played by Elisabeth Rohm), and Executive Assistant DA Jack McCoy (played by Sam Waterston). These characters went through some tough times—Briscoe battled alcoholism, Green was shot in the line of duty, Southerlyn struggled with homophobia, and McCoy dealt with corruption charges—but they always came out on top in the end. That made them not only great characters but also great role models.

Another thing that made Law & Order so great was the stories. Every episode began with a crime, usually a murder, and then followed the detectives as they tried to solve it. This was intercut with scenes from the trial, giving viewers a front-row seat to both the investigation and the prosecution. And just when you thought you had figured out who did it, there would be a twist that completely changed everything. It was always exciting, always unpredictable, and always entertaining.

## Married with Children - Comedy - 1987 - 1997

"Married with Children" was one of the first sitcoms to show that families aren't perfect. Until then, most sitcoms depicted families as these idealized units that always got along and never argued. But "Married with Children" showed that families fight and argue like everyone else. And while they sometimes drove each other crazy, at the end of the day, they loved each other unconditionally.

Personally, I was a big fan of Peggy Bundy, played by Katey Segal. The show "Married with Children" may have only aired for 11 seasons—but it has left a lasting impression on American culture.

The show has been praised by critics and is often cited as one of the most influential sitcoms of all time. In 2009, it even entered the Guinness World Records as the longest-running live-action comedy series with 262 episodes! There's no doubt about it: "Married with Children" is a true cult classic.

## Buffy the Vampire Slayer - 1997 - 2003

I bet you were also a fan of Sarah Michelle Gellar! She was responsible for the huge fan following the show had, as well as teen girls crushing on Angel.

Buffy the Vampire Slayer was more than just a TV show; it was a revolution. It empowered women, showing us that girls can be strong and independent. For example, in most horror movies, women are helpless victims who spend most of their time running and screaming from whatever monster is chasing them. But in Buffy, it was always the monsters that ended up running and screaming from Buffy. She wasn't afraid to fight back and quickly proved that girls could be just as badass as any boy.

The show depicted women's friendship realistically, and it even managed to be hilarious and scary simultaneously. If you've never seen Buffy the Vampire Slayer, now is the perfect time to start watching. Trust me; you won't regret it!

**Full House - 1987 - 1995**

Full House was a family-friendly show appropriate for audiences of all ages. If you were a child of the 90s, chances are you grew up watching the hit TV show Full House. The show aired from 1987 to 1995. It was about a widowed father who is raising his three daughters with the help of his brother-in-law and best friend. Full House was feel-good television at its finest, and it's no wonder the show is still popular today, nearly 30 years after it first aired.

Why did people love it so much? The show focused on family values. At a time when other sitcoms were filled with sex jokes and other adult humor, Full House often tackled more serious issues like peer pressure and racism in a way that was both entertaining and educational. The show also emphasized the importance of sticking together as a family, no matter the difficult times. These values are something that viewers could always rely on—and they're one of the reasons why we still love

Full House today.

## The Dinosaurs - 1991 - 1995

I used to love watching The Dinosaurs; it was such a unique show, even by today's standards. With cute quotes like "Gotta love the baby!" and "Not the Mama," it was certainly memorable.

The Dinosaurs didn't shy away from tackling important social issues, but it did so in a way that was accessible and fun for kids. In one episode, for example, the family deals with environmentalism after they realize that they're polluting the Earth. In another episode, they learn about gender equality when grandmother Ethel gets a job and earns her own money. These are complex issues, but The Dinosaurs made them approachable for younger viewers without talking down to them.

## Saved By The Bell - 1989 - 1993

Saved by the Bell was more than just a TV show; it was a cultural phenomenon. Thanks to its lovable characters and hilarious plotlines, Saved by the Bell captured viewers' hearts everywhere and continues to be one of the most popular shows of all time. This show gave us a glimpse into high school in the '90s. All the girls were crushing on Zach, and the guys watching the show had the hots for Kelly.

Whether you were Team Zack or Team Slater, there was no denying that the cast of Saved By The Bell was charming. They were also pretty diverse, which was refreshing for a '90s sitcom. There was the token nerd (Screech), the rich girl (Lisa), the jock (Slater), the transfer student (Zack), and even a couple of adults (Mr. Belding and Miss Bliss). Everyone had their own quirks and foibles, but they were ultimately likable—and that's what made us keep tuning in week after week.

## The Fresh Prince of Bel-Air - 1990 - 1996

This is the show that skyrocketed Will Smith's acting career because it was wildly popular. The Fresh Prince of Bel-Air was a sitcom that aired on NBC from 1990 to 1996. The show followed the antics of a street-wise teenager from Philadelphia named Will Smith, who is sent to live with his wealthy aunt and uncle in Bel-Air, California. The show was famous for its light-hearted humor, 90s fashion, and memorable catchphrases. But what made The Fresh Prince of Bel-Air great was its ability to tackle difficult topics in a way that was accessible to its young audience.

In many ways, The Fresh Prince of Bel-Air was ahead of its time. It was one of the first mainstream television shows to deal with issues like racism, police brutality, and teen pregnancy in a way that didn't preach to its audience or talk down to them. Instead, the show used humor and relatable characters to get its points across. As a result, The Fresh Prince of Bel-Air became one of the most popular shows of the '90s.

## Friends - 1994 - 2004

If you grew up in the '90s, then there's a good chance you were a big fan of the sitcom Friends. The show, which ran for ten seasons from 1994 to 2004, was must-see TV for many people during that time. Even now, more than 15 years after it ended, Friends remains one of the most popular TV shows of all time. But what made it so great?

The cast was terrific. From Jennifer Aniston (Rachel) to Courteney Cox (Monica) to Lisa Kudrow (Phoebe), each member of the Friends cast brought their own unique talents and personality to the show. This helped make the characters feel like real people that viewers could relate to.

Overall, the show was simply iconic. From its unforgettable moments ( we're looking at you," Smelly Cat") to its catchphrases ("How you doin'?"), FRIENDS is a TV sitcom that truly has it all."

## Jerry Springer - 1991 - 2018

I don't know about you, but I couldn't wait to get home after school to see what drama was happening on Jerry Springer!

In the '90s, no TV show was more talked about than Jerry Springer. Love it or hate it, everyone had an opinion on The Jerry Springer Show. And while it's easy to look back on the show and see it as a trashy spectacle, there's no denying it was must-see TV in its day. Here's a look at why Jerry Springer was great in the '90s.

In the '90s, reality TV was still a relatively new phenomenon. And while there were a few "reality" shows on TV at the time, they were nothing like The Jerry Springer Show. On Jerry Springer, people were free to air their dirty laundry in front of a national audience with no filter. Nothing was off-limits from cheating spouses to secret love affairs on Jerry Springer. And viewers loved it!

Whether you loved or hated The Jerry Springer Show, there's no denying that it was highly entertaining. From the now-famous "Jerry!Jerry!Jerry!" chant to the outlandish guests and fights, Jerry Springer always had something going on. Even if you disagreed with what was happening on the show, you couldn't help but be captivated by it.

## Other Popular Hit TV Shows in the '90s

While I can't cover all the great ones in this short book, let's list a few more that you may have known and loved.

- Seinfield
- Twin Peaks
- Dawsons Creek
- Baywatch
- Frasier
- Boy Meets World
- Sex and the City
- Charmed
- Beverly Hills 90210
- Sabrina the Teenage Witch
- X Files
- The King of Queens
- 7th Heaven
- Oz
- Sister Sister

# 4

# Iconic Cartoons

I f you grew up in the '90s, chances are you have fond memories of watching Saturday morning cartoons. I certainly remember Nickelodeon ruling my life as a kid at this time.

The '90s was a magical time for cartoons. It was the golden age of animation, and so many iconic shows aired during that decade. From "The Simpsons" to "Ren and Stimpy," there were countless classics that we all grew up watching.

Creativity flourished, and studios were taking risks with new and innovative ideas. As a result, the '90s saw the birth of some of the most beloved animated cartoons and films of all time. They weren't afraid to experiment with new styles and genres, leading to some groundbreaking work. Another thing that made '90s animation so special was the camaraderie between the different studios. Although they were all fiercely competitive, there was also a sense of harmony and mutual respect. This led to memorable crossover projects, such as "Batman: The Animated Series" and "Tiny Toon Adventures."

But which ones were the best? Here are some top cartoons you might remember from childhood.

### Doug (1991-1994)

"Doug" was a Nickelodeon show about an 11-year-old boy named Doug Funnie who had just moved to a new town called Bluffington. Doug kept a journal where he would write down his adventures with his friends, including Skeeter Valentine, Roger Klotz, and Patty Mayonnaise. While it was definitely one of the more low-key shows on this list, it was still a lot of fun to watch.

### Dexter's Laboratory (1992-1995)

"Dexter's Laboratory" was one of Cartoon Network's first breakout hits. It followed the misadventures of a boy genius named Dexter, who had his own secret laboratory where he would invent all sorts of crazy devices. Unfortunately for Dexter, his sister Dee Dee would always find her way into his laboratory and ruin his experiments. It was a very creative show with some wacky episodes.

### Rocko's Modern Life (1993-1996)

Nickelodeon's "Rocko's Modern Life" follows the everyday life of an Australian wallaby named Rocko, who has to deal with all sorts of wacky situations. From dealing with his next-door neighbor Mr Bighead to working atCOMICS!." Rocko's Modern Life" is full of absurdist humor that will leave you laughing out loud. It's one of Nickelodeon's most underrated shows from the '90s.

### The Simpsons (1989 - Current)

No list of iconic '90s cartoons would be complete without "The Simpsons." The show first aired in 1989, but it didn't hit its stride until the early '90s. By 1993, "The Simpsons" was the most-watched show on television, and it held that title for several years. Even today, it remains one of the most popular shows on TV. What makes "The Simpsons" so unique? It could be the lovable (if dysfunctional) family at the show's center, or the clever humor that appeals to both kids and adults. Whatever the reason, there's no denying that "The Simpsons" is one of the most popular cartoons of all time.

## SpongeBob SquarePants (1999 - Current)

Another cartoon that achieved widespread popularity in the '90s was "SpongeBob SquarePants." The show debuted in 1999 and quickly became a hit with kids and adults alike. Its mix of humor, colorful characters, and catchy songs made it an instant classic. "SpongeBob" is still going strong today, with a movie released in 2020 and more planned for the future. There's no doubt that this lovable sea sponge will continue to delight audiences for years to come.

## South Park (1997 - Current)

It's been almost 25 years since South Park first aired on Comedy Central, and in that time, the show has become nothing short of a pop culture phenomenon. From its humble beginnings as a crudely animated satire of small-town America to its current status as one of the most intelligent and biting social commentaries on television, South Park has come a long way. Here are a few reasons why South Park was the greatest show of the 90s.

First, it was unapologetically crude. In an era where political correctness was beginning to take hold, South Park was a breath of fresh air. The show didn't pull any punches regarding its satire, and it was all the better for it. Whether they were taking on religious hypocrisy or media sensationalism, South Park always went for the jugular.

The show had no feat of controversy. In today's climate of cancel culture, it's hard to imagine a show like South Park being able to get away with half of the things it did in the 90s. But back then, controversies only made the show more popular. From its earliest episodes, South Park has never shied away from touchy subjects, or the willingness to tackle taboo topics which makes the show so great.

## Rugrats (1991 - 2004)

The Rugrats was a popular cartoon in the 90s for various reasons. For one, it featured an adorable cast of characters like Tommy and Chucky that kids could easily relate to. Personally, I loved Angelica!

Another reason the show was appealing is that it had a unique sense of humor that appealed to both adults and children. Additionally, the Rugrats tackled a wide range of topics, from the first time a baby gets a haircut to the fears of starting school. This helped to make the show relatable for viewers of all ages.

Lastly, the Rugrats had great chemistry and always managed to find themselves in the middle of wacky adventures. All of these factors came together to make the Rugrats a timeless classic still beloved by fans today.

## Barney (1992 - 2010)

This one is quite fun to look back on. It's the classic show everyone watched, but no one admitted to watching. Few TV shows have captured kids' imagination in the way that Barney did in the early 1990s. The big purple dinosaur was an instant hit with his sing-along songs and positive message, "I Love You." What's not to love? For kids, Barney was a larger-than-life character who they could look up to. He was always cheerful and optimistic, even when things got tough. And he always had time for a hug (or several). It's no wonder that Barney quickly became one of the most popular characters on TV. For many kids growing up in the 1990s, Barney was a beloved part of their childhood.

## Blue's Clues (1996 - 2006)

Blue's Clues was a popular Nickelodeon cartoon that aired in the late 1990s. I was a little outside of the targeted age range by the time this one came out, but it was still cute nonetheless. The show followed the exploits of a puppy named Blue and her human friend, Steve. One of the things that made the show so successful was its innovative format.

Each episode began with Steve receiving a clue from Blue, which he would then use to solve a puzzle. This simple premise allowed for a wide variety of creative and educational content. In addition, the show's interactive elements encouraged viewers to participate in the solving of each puzzle. As a result, Blue's Clues became one of the most popular shows on television during its six-year run.

## Captain Planet (1990 - 1996)

The '90s was a decade that was filled with change. One of the most significant changes was how people saw the environment. In the past, the environment was often seen as an infinite resource that could be used without consequence.

However, in the '90s, people began to wake up to the reality of climate change and environmental destruction. Against this backdrop, Captain Planet and the Planeteers became a popular cartoon show. The show follows the adventures of a group of teens who a wise Gaia gives superpowers. They use their powers to protect the planet from eco-villains who are looking to exploit its resources. As a result, Captain Planet was able to tap into the growing concern over environmental issues and become a popular show in the '90s.

Captain Planet was such a dope show about saving the environment. But, myself and my cousins would even make a game out of it, and we would get rings from the 50-cent machines and pretend we got special powers.

## Courage The Cowardly Dog (1996 - 2002)

The show was full of surprises, and no two episodes were ever alike. This made it very exciting to watch and always left viewers wanting more. Another reason Courage the Cowardly Dog was so great is its unique sense of humor. This made it very enjoyable to watch and helped set it apart from other cartoons of the time. Each episode taught valuable lessons about life, relationships, and overcoming fears.

The show not only entertaining but also educational. All these factors combined make Courage the Cowardly Dog one of the best cartoons of the 90s. Personally, what I loved about Courage The Cowardly Dog is that the old people reminded me of my own grandparents.

## Other Popular Cartoons Shows in the '90s

- The Powerpuff Girls
- Arthur
- Bevis and Butthead
- Johnny Bravo
- The Angry Beavers
- The Wild Thornberrys
- Animaniacs
- Pinky and the Brain
- Bobby's World

# 5

# Iconic Movies

D uring the '90s movie theaters and video rental was thriving. It was a little different than what we know today as Netflix and chill, but not completely different. People loved to go out on dates and watch a movie at the theater or rent a movie for the weekend for the family. I remember going on dates when I was sixteen to the local AMC. Clearly, people loved movies in the '90s, but what cultivated that obsession?

Let's travel back in time, and review some of the amazing advancements in filmmaking. New technologies such as CGI (computer-generated imagery) and Dolby Digital sound were used to create more immersive movie experiences. During this time we also saw the birth of the DVD format, which would eventually replace VHS tapes as the preferred way to watch movies at home.

Another factor that made movies great in the 1990s was the abandonment of the Hays Code. This code was implemented in 1930 and dictated what could and could not be shown on screen. For example, any depiction of illegal activities or "immoral" behavior was strictly forbidden. The code was slowly relaxed over time, but it wasn't until the 1990s that it was finally abandoned altogether. This allowed filmmakers to explore more mature themes and push the boundaries of what could be shown on screen.

The 1990s also saw a resurgence in animated films. After a decade or two of live-action domination, Disney regained its footing with The Little Mermaid, Beauty and the Beast, Aladdin, and Toy Story. Pixar would also debut in 1995 with Toy Story, which would become one of the most popular and influential animated films ever made. Thanks to Disney and Pixar, animated films were once again a staple at your local theater.

Hollywood was also getting more extreme. A new generation of filmmakers, actors, and actresses emerged, who would go on to make some of the most iconic films of all time. These included directors like Quentin Tarantino and Tim Burton; actors like Leonardo DiCaprio, Tom Hanks, and Brad Pitt; and actresses like Jennifer Aniston, Julia Roberts, and Cameron Diaz. Together, they helped create a new Golden Age of Hollywood that would produce some truly great films.

But, there is still more to the story as to what drove the obsession to go to the movies every weekend. Changes also occurred in the way that movies were marketed. Previously, studios relied heavily on television commercials to promote their latest releases. However, in the 1990s, they began to use the Internet to reach potential audiences. This new form of marketing allowed them to reach a wider audience and connect with viewers on a more personal level. As a result, the 1990s were a decade of great change for the movie industry.

Although compared to today, our love of movies did not change, just how we have access to them. But, there is something nostalgic about going to the dollar tree to stock up on snacks before going to the dollar movie theater to do entertainment on a budget in the '90s.

Let's reflect on some of our favorite movies from the 90s!

*P.S. Let me apologize in advance for not getting all the great ones on this list; Clearly, there is just too much to cover in this section!*

## Hocus Pocus (1993)

I'm adding Hocus Pocus to the top of this list because it's nearly 30 years later, and they just released Hocus Pocus 2! Part of the reason this Halloween classic has so much popularity is that it's a film that can be enjoyed again and again, no matter how old you are. Here are a few reasons why "Hocus Pocus" is still popular today.

One of the things that make Hocus Pocus so appealing is the characters. The movie centers around three witches: Bette Midler as Winifred Sanderson, Kathy Najimy as Mary Sanderson, and Sarah Jessica Parker as Sarah Sanderson. These three actresses play their roles to perfection and have great on-screen chemistry. It's hard not to root for them, even though they are technically the movie's villains.

Halloween can be scary for some people, so it's nice to have a movie that injects some fun into the holiday. Hocus Pocus is filled with hilarious moments, whether it's Winifred trying to figure out how to use a vacuum cleaner or Sarah acting like a chicken. The humor is appropriate for all ages, which is one of the reasons why the movie has such broad appeal.

## Half Baked (1998)

In the late 1990s, stoner comedies were all the rage. So, it's no surprise that the 1998 movie Half Baked rose to popularity. Starring Dave Chappelle, Jim Breuer, Harland Williams, and Guillermo Díaz, Half Baked follows the misadventures of three pothead friends who get caught selling weed stolen from a pharmaceutical lab. Despite being panned by critics, the movie was a box office success, grossing over $18 million on a budget of just $5 million.

## The Blair Witch Project (1999)

The Blair Witch Project is a horror movie that was released in 1999, and it felt so real. The movie was a found footage-style movie about three student filmmakers who disappeared in the woods while trying to make a documentary about the local legend of the Blair Witch. The film became very popular and was a box-office success. So, why was the movie so popular?

The movie was successful because it could tap into people's fears. The found footage style of the movie made it feel like it could be real, and people were scared by the idea of being lost in the woods with a deadly witch. No one wanted to go camping after watching that movie!

## Happy Gilmore (1996)

Happy Gilmore was so famous that it's still talked about today. In fact, it's often cited as one of the most quotable movies of all time. So what is it about this Adam Sandler comedy that has resonated with audiences for so long?

Happy Gilmore has stood the test of time because it's ultimately a feel-good story. Sure, it starts out with Happy being down on his luck. He's about to lose his grandmother's house, and he doesn't have any apparent talents or skills to fall back on. But through sheer determination (and a little bit of luck), he discovered his hidden golf talent and has an incredible career on the pro circuit. He even managed to save his grandmother's house in the process!

Happy Gilmore is the perfect example of a movie that will make you laugh, cry, and feel good by the time the credits roll. It's a feel-good story for the ages that continues to resonate with audiences 25 years later. So if you haven't seen it yet (or if you just want to relive some childhood nostalgia), be sure to check out Happy Gilmore today! You won't be disappointed.

## Tommy Boy (1995)

In 1995, Chris Farley and David Spade teamed up for the movie Tommy Boy. The story of an incompetent heir to an auto parts empire, Tommy Boy was a box office hit, grossing over $50 million on a $15 million budget. But what about this movie has made it such a cult classic?

Chris Farley was known for his physical comedy, and Tommy Boy is full of his signature slapstick. From tumbling down a flight of stairs to getting hit in the crotch, Farley's willingness to do anything for a laugh is on full display in this film. And while some of the gags might be considered crass by today's standards, they're still hilariously funny.

One of the main reasons why Tommy Boy has such a devoted following is that it is relatable. Farley's character may be the heir to an auto parts empire, but he is entirely unprepared to run the business. He is naïve, accident-prone, and completely lacking in common sense. In other words, he is someone in which many people can see themselves.

Tommy Boy remains one of the most popular comedies of all time, thanks to its mix of physical comedy, deadpan delivery, and heartwarming message. If you've never seen it, do yourself a favor and check it out—you won't be disappointed.

## American Pie (1999)

Ask anyone born in the 1990s about their favorite teen movie, and you're likely to hear the same answer again and again: American Pie. The film, which follows a group of high school friends trying to lose their virginity on prom night, was an instant classic when it was released in 1999.

It drew us in with insightful observations about teenage sexuality. When it comes to discussing sex, teenagers are often portrayed as either naively innocent or ragingly hormonal. American Pie, however, took a more nuanced approach to the subject.

The film's characters deal with their sexuality more thoughtfully, touching on everything from awkward virginities to unexpected erections. This realistic depiction of teenage sexuality was a breath of fresh air for many viewers, who could finally see themselves represented on-screen.

## Men In Black (1997)

If you were a kid in the '90s, chances are good that you were obsessed with the Men in Black franchise. The original film, released in 1997, was an instant hit with audiences of all ages, and its sequel only added to the hype. But what was it about these movies that made them so popular?

In a world where blockbusters are often cookie-cutter copies of other successful films, it's refreshing to come across a movie with a completely original concept. Men in Black is about a secret government organization that monitors and regulates extraterrestrial activity on Earth. This high-concept plotline was unlike anything audiences had seen before, and it's one of the main reasons the film was so successful.

The film featured Will Smith and Tommy Lee Jones as the titular men in black, two actors who were already household names thanks to their work on television shows like The Fresh Prince of Bel-Air and Home Improvement. Add in other big names like Rip Torn and Vincent D'Onofrio; you've got a recipe for success.

The Special Effects Were Out of This World, literally! At a time when CGI was still in its infancy, the special effects used in Men in Black were truly ahead of their time. The film's aliens were created using puppetry, animatronics, and computer-generated imagery, and they looked so realistic that audiences were convinced they were real! Coupled with some incredible action sequences, it's no wonder people couldn't get enough of this movie.

## The Sandlot (1993)

For many people of a certain age, the 1993 film The Sandlot is synonymous with summer. The coming-of-age story about a group of neighborhood kids who play baseball together every day captured the attention of 90s kids across the country and quickly became a cult classic. But what is it about The Sandlot that has made it endure for so long?

A big part of what makes The Sandlot so unique is its portrayal of childhood friendships. The movie captures the magic and joy of those carefree days when the only thing that mattered was playing ball with your friends. It's a feeling that many people can relate to and one that continues to resonate with viewers today.

## Speed (1994)

In the 1990s, action movies were all the rage. Films like Die Hard, Arnold Schwarzenegger's Total Recall, and Luc Besson's The Fifth Element were box office gold. But of all the action movies released in the '90s, none was more popular than Jan de Bont's Speed. Starring Keanu Reeves and Sandra Bullock, Speed was a critical and commercial success, grossing $350 million on a budget of $30 million. So, what made the film so popular?

Speed is packed with heart-pounding action scenes that keep audiences on the edge of their seats. From the opening scene—in which an elevator full of people slowly starts to drop—to the climactic finale—in which Jack and company must outrun a massive explosion—the film is nonstop thrills from beginning to end. De Bont, who also served as the film's cinematographer, did an incredible job of making each action set piece look stunning on screen.

From its simple yet exciting plot to its lovable yet unlikely characters, there are so many things to love about Speed. It's no wonder this movie was such a hit in the '90s—and remains popular even today. So if you're looking for a fast-paced thrill ride of a movie, look no further than Speed. You won't be disappointed.

## Home Alone (1990)

If you were a kid growing up in the '90s, chances are good that you spent at least one winter break watching Home Alone on repeat. But what made this movie so popular? Was it the hilarious hijinks of precocious youngster Kevin McCallister? The boundless energy of Macaulay Culkin? The impeccable comedic timing of director Chris Columbus? Actually, it was probably all of those things—and more.

One of the most obvious reasons it was popular is because the movie was relatable and funny—really funny. From Macaulay Culkin's deadpan delivery of lines like "Keep the change, ya filthy animal" to Joe Pesci's over-the-top characterizations of Harry and Marv, there was plenty of comic relief throughout the movie. Even now, nearly 30 years later, I can't watch Home Alone without laughing out loud at least once.

Whether you watch it every year during the holidays or only pull it out every once in awhile, there's no denying that Home Alone is a classic film. So what makes this movie so special? Its relatable plotline, hilarious comedy, and sense of wonderment are just a few of the reasons why Home Alone continues to charm audiences generation after generation.

## Mrs. Doubtfire (1993)

Mrs. Doubtfire and the movie remains just as popular as it was when it first came out. Robin Williams gives a fantastic performance as Daniel Hillard, a struggling actor who pretends to be a woman so he can get a job as his ex-wife's nanny and spend more time with his kids. The movie is funny, heartwarming, and relatable, which is why we still love it today.

One of the things that make Mrs. Doubtfire so great is that it's hilarious while also touching and sentimental. The movie never takes itself too seriously, but it also doesn't shy away from some of the more challenging aspects of divorce and single parenting. Daniel is a great father who loves his kids unconditionally, which comes through loud and clear in every scene he's in with them. The movie is funny, heartwarming, and relatable, which is why we still love it today.

## Other Popular Movies from the '90s

- Forrest Gump
- Dumb & Dumber
- Total Recall
- The Sixth Sense
- Edward Scissorhands
- Beauty and the Beast
- Seven
- The Professional
- Pretty Woman
- Clerks
- The Silence of The Lambs
- Toy Story
- Good Will Hunting
- Groundhog Day
- Scream
- Goodfellas
- Clueless
- Friday
- Fight Club
- The Matrix
- Jurassic Park
- Titanic

- The Lion King
- Pulp Fiction
- The Shawshank Redemption

# 6

# Music in the '90s

L et's talk about music in the 90s. It's no secret that music today isn't what it used to be. In fact, many people argue that music peaked in the '90s and has been downhill ever since. While there's no way to definitively say whether or not that's true, there are certainly some elements of '90s music that can't be found in today's hits.

It was a time when the industry was in flux, and new genres were being created every day. From grunge to techno, there was something for everyone. The 90s saw the rise of some truly talented artists. Madonna, Michael Jackson, Nirvana, Pearl Jam, and Mariah Carey are just a few of the iconic musicians who emerged during this decade.

Throughout this decade, we experienced a major transition in the industry. The music industry was evolving by leaps and bounds. Music videos became super popular and were truly innovative. Directors like Spike Jonze and Michel Gondry pushed the boundaries of what was possible with music videos, and their creativity helped shape the industry's future.

Not only was the music innovative, but the technology for the delivery of music was also changing. We started shifting from buying cassettes to buying CDs. We began to trade our boomboxes for portable CD players. The music shifted again as MP3s gained popularity, and by the end of the decade, a new portable music player was born…the MP3 player. So over ten years, we went from recording songs on the radio to our cassette tapes to downloading MP3s off the internet to burn CDs, and then jumping right into getting our hands on the latest tech of MP3 players at the time.

# 7

# Iconic Songs

**W**aterfalls by TLC - 1994

In the mid-1990s, one song dominated the airwaves. It was a catchy tune with a message about society's ills, and it spent seven weeks atop the Billboard Hot 100 chart. That song was "Waterfalls" by TLC, and 25 years later, it's still popular.

The lyrics to "Waterfalls" offer a harsh reality check about some of society's biggest issues: drug dealing, gangs, violence, and disease. But despite all that heavy subject matter, the song's overall message is one of hope and perseverance. TLC encourages listeners to stay strong in the face of adversity and resist temptation because "those things only bring you down." It's a message that resonated with listeners in 1995 and continues to do so today.

## The Sign by Ace of Base - 1992

In the early '90s, there was no escaping Ace of Base's "The Sign." The Swedish group's debut single was inescapable on radio and MTV, and it spent six weeks atop the Billboard Hot 100. All of those years later, the song remains popular, regularly appearing on best-of lists and getting covered by other artists. But what made "The Sign" so special?

One of the reasons "The Sign" was so successful was because of its catchy melody. The song's opening riff is instantly recognizable, and it's the kind of earworm that gets stuck in your head for days on end. Even if you're not a fan of the lyrics, there's no denying that the melody is catchy and easy to sing along to.

In addition to having a catchy melody and universal lyrics, "The Sign" also had an iconic music video. The video starred Jenny Berggren as a woman who travels around the world spreading joy and positivity wherever she goes. It was uplifting and feel-good, perfectly matching the song's tone. Plus, it didn't hurt that Jenny Berggren was absolutely gorgeous.

## Smooth by Santana - 1999

In 1999, the song "Smooth" by Santana featuring Rob Thomas of Matchbox Twenty was released. The song was everywhere in 1999-2000, spending 12 weeks at the top of the Billboard Hot 100 chart and ultimately winning three Grammy Awards, including Record of the Year.

Here's a little history for ya! The song was actually released in 1999, but it didn't start getting significant airplay until early 2000. Santana had been working on a comeback album and needed a hit single to jumpstart sales. He initially asked Matchbox Twenty frontman, Rob Thomas, to write a song with him, but Thomas was too busy working on his own album. However, he did have a demo of a song he had written that he thought might be a good fit for Santana. That song was "Smooth."

After hearing the demo, Santana knew he wanted to record it. However, Thomas was reluctant to give up the song entirely, so they decided to record it as a duet.

## U Can't Touch This by MC Hammer - 1990

At the time, the song was inescapable; it was played on the radio constantly, and its music video was in heavy rotation on MTV. Even today, the song is instantly recognizable and remains a favorite among fans of '90s hip-hop. But what about this particular song has made it endure for so long?

One of the things that make "U Can't Touch This" so catchy is its use of Rick James' 1981 hit, "Super Freak." The unforgettable bass line provides the perfect backdrop for Hammer's lyrics and ensures that the song gets stuck in your head after just one listen. In fact, the use of Rick James' sample was so integral to the song's success that James was given a co-writing credit.

On another note, its sheer energy makes "U Can't Touch This" such a timeless classic. From start to finish, the song is high-octane fun. There's no doubt that Hammer himself was having a blast making this song, and that sense of joy is contagious. You can't help but smile when you hear it.

## Baby One More Time - 1998

In the late 1990s, a new pop sensation took the world by storm. Her name was Britney Spears, and her debut single "Baby One More Time" became an instant smash hit. To this day, the song remains one of the most popular songs of all time. But what is it about "Baby One More Time" that has made it such a classic?

For starters, "Baby One More Time" was so popular because of its controversial music video. The video featured Britney dressed in a schoolgirl uniform and dancing provocatively in a Catholic school setting. While some critics denounced the video as too suggestive for younger viewers, others praised its artistic merit. Love it or hate it, there's no denying that the video helped make "Baby One More Time" take off.

**Bitter Sweet Symphony by The Verve - 1997**

The song was everywhere—on the radio, TV, and in movies. It even won a Grammy!

One of the things that makes "Bitter Sweet Symphony" so special is the lyrics. Written by lead singer Richard Ashcroft, the lyrics are profound and poetic, with a message that resonates with people worldwide. The song's opening lines, "'Cause it's a bitter sweet symphony, this life/Tryin' to make ends meet, you're a slave to money then you die," perfectly captures the human experience of struggling to get by in a world that often seems unfair.

Perhaps one of the most controversial aspects of "Bitter Sweet Symphony" is the fact that it was used in a commercial without permission. In 1997, Nike released an ad featuring NFL star Jerry Rice set to the tune of "Bitter Sweet Symphony." The Verve was not happy about it and sued for copyright infringement. While they eventually settled out of court, Ashcroft has said that he still feels like he didn't get proper credit for his work. Nevertheless, the controversy surrounding the song only added to its popularity.

## Wannabe by Spice Girls - 1996

The 1990s were a decade of many firsts. One of those firsts was the debut of the girl group known as the Spice Girls. The group, consisting of Melanie Brown ("Scary Spice"), Melanie Chisholm ("Sporty Spice"), Emma Bunton ("Baby Spice"), Geri Halliwell ("Ginger Spice"), and Victoria Beckham (formerly "Posh Spice"), became a global phenomenon with their catchy songs, infectious energy, and girl power message. One of their most popular songs, "Wannabe," was released in 1996 and quickly topped charts around the world.

One of the main reasons "Wannabe" was so successful is because of its melody. The song's main hook—"if you wanna be my love, you gotta get with my friends"—is extremely catchy and easy to remember. Even if you haven't heard the song in years, chances are you can still sing along to it without skipping a beat. That's the sign of a truly great pop song.

In addition to having great lyrics and a memorable melody, "Wannabe" also features some funky production elements that help make it stand out from other pop songs of the era. The use of an Instagram filter on the album artwork was ahead of its time, while the heavy use of Auto-Tune on Melanie Brown's vocals gives the track a unique sound that separates it from anything else that was out at the time. These production choices helped make "Wannabe" an instant classic.

## Smells Like Teen Spirit by Nirvana - 1991

It's been over 30 years since Nirvana's "Smells Like Teen Spirit" first graced the airwaves, and the song remains as popular as ever. Though it's now widely considered one of the greatest rock songs of all time, it wasn't an instant success. In fact, when the band released it as their first single off of their second album, Nevermind, nobody could have predicted that it would go on to define a generation. So, how did a song with such humble beginnings become an anthem for millions worldwide?

The song was actually written as a parody of popular 80s hair metal bands. When asked about the inspiration for the song, lead singer Kurt Cobain said: "I was trying to write the ultimate pop song. I was basically trying to rip off the Pixies. I have to admit it."

Interestingly enough, though the song was intended as a satire, many of the bands that it was poking fun at ended up covering it. In fact, Bon Jovi's Richie Sambora has said that he wishes his band had been the ones to record it because he thinks it would have been a huge hit for them. Regardless of its origins, there's no denying that "Smells Like Teen Spirit" struck a chord with people all over the world.

### Baby Got Back by Sir Mix-a-Lot - 1992

Sir Mix-a-Lot's "Baby Got Back" is undoubtedly one of the most controversial songs of the 1990s. The song, which celebrates curvy women, was accused of being misogynistic and demeaning to women. However, there is more to the song than meets the eye. In fact, "Baby Got Back" was considered to be a celebration of female empowerment and body-positivity.

Now, I know what you're thinking: How can a song with lyrics like "I like big butts, and I cannot lie" be empowering to women? But When

Sir Mix-a-Lot wrote "Baby Got Back," he made a statement about the mainstream media's portrayal of beauty. At the time, the media was obsessed with stick-thin supermodels like Cindy Crawford and Christy Turlington. Sir Mix-a-Lot wanted to celebrate women with curves, and he did so in a fun and catchy way.

### Everybody by Backstreet Boys - 1997

Boy bands were all the rage in the late 1990s and early 2000s. Among the most popular of these groups was the Backstreet Boys, whose debut album "Backstreet's Back" propelled them to superstardom. The lead single off of that album was "Everybody (Backstreet's Back)," a catchy tune that quickly became a sensation.

The song was released in July 1997 as the lead single from the group's self-titled debut album. It was an instant hit, debuting at #4 on the Billboard Hot 100 chart and ultimately reaching #1 in 15 countries. The music video for the song was also a big hit, receiving heavy rotation on MTV and other music video channels.

So what made "Everybody (Backstreet's Back)" so popular? There are a few factors that likely contributed to its success. First, the song is incredibly catchy and easy to sing along to. Second, the accompanying music video is very well-done and entertaining. Finally, the song came at a time when boy bands were really beginning to take off in popularity, so it tapped into that zeitgeist perfectly.

### Other Throwback Songs from the '90s

- Good Vibrations by Loleatta Holloway - 1991

- Are You That Somebody by Aaliyah - 1998
- Iris by Goo Goo Dolls - 1998
- Don't Speak by No Doubt - 1995
- MMMBop by Hanson - 1997
- Losing My Religion by R.E.M. - 1991
- Barbie Girl by Aqua - 1997
- Un-Break My Heart by Toni Braxton - 1996
- Truly Madly Deeply by Savage Garden - 1997
- Always Be My Baby by Mariah Carey - 1995
- Linger by The Cranberries - 1993
- My Heart Will Go On by Celine Dion - 1997
- The Rain by Miss Elliott - 1997
- Self Esteem by The Offspring - 1994
- Wonderwall by Oasis - 1995

# 8

# Influential Artists & Bands

M ariah Carey

In the 1990s, Mariah Carey was one of the world's most prolific and successful recording artists. A string of hit singles, including " Vision of Love," "Emotions," and "My All," made her one of the most popular singers of the decade. Take a look at Mariah Carey's incredible career in the 1990s.

Mariah Carey got her start in the music industry in 1988 when she met record producer Mutt Lange. Carey would go on to release her self-titled debut album in 1990. The album was an instant success, spawning four number-one singles on the Billboard Hot 100 chart. With her debut album, Mariah Carey quickly established herself as a force to be reckoned with in the music industry.

In 1991, Mariah Carey released her second album, Emotions. The album was another huge success, debuting at number one on the Billboard 200 chart and selling over eight million copies in the United States alone. The album's lead single, "Emotions," became one of Carey's signature songs and solidified her status as one of the biggest pop stars in the world.

Throughout the rest of the 1990s, Mariah Carey continued to release hit after hit, cementing her place as one of the best-selling music artists of all time. In 1998, she released her fifth studio album, Butterfly. The album debuted at number one on the Billboard 200 chart and spawned two number-one singles, "Honey" and "My All." Carey ended the decade with a bang when she collaborated with Whitney Houston on the song "When You Believe" for The Prince of Egypt soundtrack; the song won an Academy Award for Best Original Song.

## Madonna

Madonna was everywhere. She was on the radio, on MTV, and in magazines. She was one of the most popular singers of her time, and her popularity only increased in the 1990s. Madonna's look and sound were constantly evolving, which kept her fans engaged. She also wasn't afraid to push boundaries, which helped her to stand out from other artists of her time. Let's look at some reasons why Madonna was such a diva in the 1990s.

One of the things that made Madonna so famous in the 1990s was her willingness to push boundaries. She wasn't afraid to experiment with her image and always seemed ahead of the curve. For example, in 1991, she released the book "Sex" which featured nude photos of herself. This book caused quite a stir and solidified Madonna as a provocateur. In 1992, she appeared on David Letterman wearing a wedding dress and then flashed him during an interview. This interview caused even more controversy and increased Madonna's popularity. Madonna knew how to get people talking and used that to her advantage.

She was constantly evolving. Her look, sound, and image were always changing, which kept her fans engaged. Madonna never rested on her laurels; she was always trying something new. For example, in 1990, she released the album "Like a Prayer" which featured a more mature sound than her previous albums. In 1995, she released the album "Bedtime Stories," which featured a more R&B sound than anything she had done before. And in 1998, she released the album "Ray of Light," which featured a more electronic sound than anything she had done before. Each new album surprised and delighted her fans who were always eager to see what she would do next.

## Michael Jackson

During this decade, there was no more prominent name in music than Michael Jackson. The self-proclaimed "King of Pop" released a string of hit albums and singles that cemented his place as one of the greatest entertainers of all time. From the release of "Dangerous" in 1991 to his Super Bowl XXXVI halftime show performance in 2002, Jackson's artistry and showmanship knew no bounds. Here's a look back at some of the most significant moments of Jackson's career in the 1990s.

During the 1990s, Jackson won numerous awards for his music, including three Grammy Awards and eight Billboard Music Awards. He also received recognition for his charitable work; in 1992, he was awarded an honorary doctorate from Bard College for his contributions to the arts and humanities. In 1996, he was inducted into both the Songwriters Hall of Fame and the Rock & Roll Hall of Fame.

Jackson was also honored with various lifetime achievement awards during this time period. In 1993, he received The Legend Award at the Soul Train Music Awards. Two years later, he was given The Lifetime

Achievement Award at the American Music Awards. And in 1999, he received The Living Legend Award at the Grammys.

In 1994, news broke that Michael Jackson had been accused of sexually abusing a 13-year-old boy. The boy's father filed a civil lawsuit against Jackson, alleging that he had molested his son and served him alcohol. After an investigation by child welfare officials cleared him of any wrongdoing, criminal charges were never filed against Jackson. However, he did settle the civil lawsuit out of court for 15 million dollars. Several other lawsuits alleging sexual abuse were filed against Jackson throughout his career; none of them were ever proven true, and he continued to deny all claims made against him until his death in 2009.

**Red Hot Chili Peppers**

The Red Hot Chili Peppers are a legendary band with a diehard fanbase. Their unique fusion of punk, rap, and funk made them stand out from the pack, and their danceable beats and irreverent lyrics kept fans coming back for more. In the 1990s, the Chili Peppers were at the height of their powers, churning out hit after hit and packing stadiums around the world. Let's take a trip down memory lane and explore what made the Chili Peppers so popular in the 90s.

The Chili Peppers were never a band to shy away from controversy. Their early hits like "Give It Away" and "Suck My Kiss" were laced with innuendo, while their album covers often featured semi-naked women. This rebellious attitude struck a chord with many fans in the 90s, who were tired of the clean-cut image of bands like New Kids on the Block and Backstreet Boys. The Chili Peppers were everything that those boy bands weren't, and their bad-boy reputation only made fans love them more.

In the early 1990s, the Red Hot Chili Peppers released a string of hits that cemented their place in music history. Songs like "Under the Bridge," "Californication," and "Scar Tissue" are still beloved by fans today and continue to get heavy rotation on classic rock radio stations. The Chili Peppers' popularity showed no signs of slowing down in the new millennium, as they continued to release chart-topping albums and sell out stadiums around the world.

## Spice Girls

The story of the Spice Girls begins in 1994 when a then-unknown group of girls auditioned for a new TV talent show called The X Factor. Though they didn't win the competition, they caught the eye of music producer Simon Fuller, who saw potential in the group and helped them get signed to a record label.

From there, things moved quickly for the Spice Girls. They released their debut single, "Wannabe," in 1996, and it quickly shot to the top of the charts in dozens of countries around the world. The follow-up singles, "Say You'll Be There" and "2 Become 1," were also huge hits, cementing the Spice Girls' status as a global phenomenon. In 1997, they released their debut album, Spice, which sold more than 20 million copies worldwide and made them one of the best-selling female groups of all time.

So what made the Spice Girls so famous? For one thing, they were very relatable; when other pop stars seemed increasingly out-of-touch, the Spice Girls were down-to-earth and approachable. They also had a unique image and style that set them apart from other girl groups at the time. And though they were marketed as "girl power" feminists, their appeal wasn't just limited to teenage girls—they had crossover appeal with boys and adults as well.

The Spice Girls' impact on pop culture is still evident today. In fact, many modern girl groups have cited them as an influence, including Little Mix and Fifth Harmony. The group's influence can also be seen in fashion; several designers have credited the Spice Girls with making platform shoes and sporty streetwear trendy in the late 1990s. And though they haven't recorded new music together in over 20 years, rumors of a reunion tour have been swirling for years—proof that even after all this time, people still can't get enough of these iconic ladies.

## Bon Jovi

Bon Jovi's popularity exploded in 1988 with the release of their fourth studio album, "New Jersey." The record was an instant smash hit, selling more than 7 million copies in the United States alone. It also spawned five top-10 singles on the Billboard Hot 100 chart, including the No. 1 hit "Bad Medicine." Suddenly, Bon Jovi was one of the biggest bands in the world.

Bon Jovi didn't slow down after releasing "New Jersey." In 1992, they came out with their fifth studio album, "Keep the Faith." The record was another huge commercial success, selling more than 5 million copies in the United States. It also contained Bon Jovi's most successful single of the 90s, "Always," which peaked at No. 4 on the Billboard Hot 100 chart.

The band took a bit of a break after releasing "Keep the Faith," but they were back in business in 1995 with their sixth studio album, "These Days." The record continued Bon Jovi's streak of commercial success, selling more than 8 million copies worldwide. It also produced several hits singles, including "This Ain't a Love Song" and "Lie to Me."

The band's mix of rock anthems and power ballads struck a chord with fans worldwide, and their concerts were always sell-outs. If you were a teenager in the 90s, chances are good that you spent at least a little bit of time jamming out to Bon Jovi.

**Rage Against The Machine**

In the 1990s, a new band emerged that would come to define the sound of an entire generation. Rage Against the Machine's unique blend of rap, rock, and metal influenced a whole new wave of music, and their politically-charged lyrics spoke to a generation of disaffected youth.

Rage Against the Machine had something for everyone. Their sound was aggressive and powerful, but it also contained elements of funk and hip-hop. This made them appealing to fans of both rock and rap music. Additionally, their lyrics were unapologetically political, which resonated with many young people who were disillusioned with the state of the world. As a result, Rage Against the Machine became one of the most popular bands of the 1990s.

In addition to their music, Rage Against the Machine was also known for their outspoken activism. The band was very critical of government policies, and they used their platform to shine a light on social injustice. Their passion for fighting for what they believed in was evident in everything they did, and this only endeared them more to their fans.

**Snoop Dogg**

If there's one rapper who epitomized the West Coast hip-hop scene of the early 1990s, it's Snoop Dogg. With his smooth flow and laid-back lyrics, Snoop quickly became a fan favorite with his debut album, "Doggystyle."

He was unapologetically himself. In an industry that is notoriously tough on artists who don't conform to mainstream norms, Snoop carved out his own niche and never wavered from it. He rapped about the things he loved—weed, women, and girls—and his unique perspective made him stand out from the rest.

Snoop worked with some of the best in the business. Throughout his career, he had the opportunity to collaborate with some of music's biggest names, including Dr. Dre, Quincy Jones, and Willie Nelson. His willingness to work with other artists showed his versatility as an artist and widened his appeal to fans of all genres.

Whether he's taking over Late Night with Jimmy Fallon or appearing in a Super Bowl commercial, Snoop is always down to have a good time. He's even been known to dabble in acting, starring in movies like "Starsky & Hutch" and "Training Day." It's clear that he doesn't take himself too seriously, and that's one of the things we love about him!

## Beastie Boys

A time when flannel was in, grunge was king, and the Beastie Boys ruled the airwaves. If you were lucky enough to come of age in this decade, then you know just how influential the Beastie Boys were.

The Beastie Boys were paving the way for a new era of rap. In the '80s, rap was still very much in its infancy. The genre was mostly confined to underground clubs and small record labels. There were a few mainstream rap hits here and there, but for the most part, rap music was still largely unknown to mainstream audiences. That all changed with the release of Licensed to Ill in 1986. This album not only shot to the top of the charts but it also introduced a whole new audience to rap music. The Beastie Boys were suddenly thrust into the spotlight and became unlikely spokespersons for a new generation of rappers.

The height of the Beastie Boys' popularity came in the early 1990s with the release of their third album, Check Your Head. Check Your Head saw the group move away from their earlier party-oriented sound and instead embrace a more experimental, hip-hop-influenced sound. The album was a commercial and critical success, cementing the Beastie Boys' place as one of the biggest bands in the world.

To say that the Beastie Boys were controversial would be an understatement. Their music was filled with profanity and references to drugs and alcohol, which earned them quite a bit of criticism from groups such as Tipper Gore's Parents Music Resource Center. But rather than shy away from their critics, the Beastie Boys embraced their bad boy image and used it to their advantage. They knew that they could use their platform to speak out against injustice and challenge societal norms—and that's exactly what they did. In 1992, they released "Sabotage," which featured a now-iconic music video that poked fun at police corruption. MTV banned the video, but that only made it more popular—and ultimately cemented the Beastie Boys' reputation as boundary-pushing radicals.

## Pearl Jam

Love them or hate them, there's no denying that Pearl Jam was one of THE biggest bands of the 1990s. With their unique blend of grunge and classic rock, Pearl Jam found a formula that resonated with fans around the world.

Pearl Jam's debut album, Ten, was released in 1991 and quickly rose to the top of the charts. Featuring hits like "Alive," "Even Flow," and "Jeremy," the album struck a chord with fans of all ages and became one of the best-selling albums of the decade. Not bad for a bunch of guys from Seattle!

In an era when many bands were fronted by larger-than-life personalities, Pearl Jam stood out as a down-to-earth group of guys who were just like their fans. They weren't afraid to show their emotions or speak their minds on issues that mattered to them, and this authenticity only endeared them more to their fans. Even today, they maintain a close connection with their fans through social media and personal appearances. It's clear that they are just as passionate about their music as they were in the 90s!

# 9

# Fashion Trends

T oday you can see hundreds of TikToks featuring classic '90s looks. The '90s were a decade of contradictions. On the one hand, we had the yin of grunge and minimalism; on the other, the yang of glamazon supermodels and sexy clubwear. Yet somehow, it all worked — thanks in part to supermodel Kate Moss, who managed to make both looks cool. (And let's not forget about Cher Horowitz's iconic style in Clueless, which defined what it meant to be "teen-appropriate" for an entire generation.)

In the earlier part of the '90s, the fashion trend was the tracksuit. Whether you were headed to the gym or just running errands, a tracksuit was a perfect choice. And you couldn't leave home without your fanny pack! Fanny packs were practical and stylish and came in all sorts of colors and patterns. They were also great for carrying around your essentials like your lip gloss, wallet, and keys—everything you need for a day on the go!

This was definitely a time period of bold fashion choices. Neon colors were all the rage, and it was not uncommon to see people wearing brightly colored tops, jackets, pants, and even shoes. If you really wanted to make a statement, you would pair your neon clothing with some acid-wash denim. Acid-wash denim was another huge trend in the 1990s and included jeans, jackets, skirts, and more.

So many unique styles emerged during this decade. Grunge fashion was popularized by Seattle-based bands like Nirvana and Pearl Jam, consisting of flannel shirts, ripped jeans, and Doc Martens boots. The grunge look was all about being comfortable and not caring too much about your appearance—a stark contrast to the flashy fashions that were popular in previous decades. If you were a teen in the '90s, chances are you owned at least one item of clothing that could be classified as "grunge."

Grudge wasn't your style? Another popular fashion trend in the 1990s was the "preppy" style, which was popularized by brands like Polo Ralph Lauren and Tommy Hilfiger. Preppy style consisted of button-down shirts, khakis, and boat shoes—basically anything that looked like it belonged on Ivy League college campuses. This trend was popular with both men and women, and it became one of the defining fashion trends of the decade.

Of course, no discussion of 90s fashion would be complete without mention of sportswear. Thanks in part to shows like "Baywatch" and movies like "Clueless," athleisure became a legitimate fashion choice in the 1990s. Suddenly it was perfectly acceptable (and even stylish) to wear tracksuits, windbreakers, and sneakers out in public. And if you were really feeling daring, you might even rock a crop top or mini skirt with your sneakers. Sportswear is still popular today, but it definitely had its moment in the spotlight in the 1990s probably why i've always preferred my sneakers!

When you think about it, the fashion of the 1990s was really unlike anything that had come before (or since). From grunge-inspired flannel to Tommy Hilfiger logos to athleisure wear, 90s fashion was truly one-of-a-kind. So whether you're nostalgic for those glory days or just curious about what people used to wear, we hope this walk down memory lane has given you some insight into one of the most unique decades in fashion history.

**Overalls**

Ah, overalls. A staple of '90s fashion (along with flannel shirts and chokers, of course). Whether you rocked denim or corduroy, there was no denying that overalls were totally cool. And they were also surprisingly versatile. You could dress them up with a tank top and heels or keep it casual with a t-shirt and sneakers. Overall, they were (pun intended) a great fashion choice. But like all trends, eventually, they faded away. So if you're feeling nostalgic for the '90s, pull out your old pair of overalls and enjoy a blast from the past.

## Headbands

Headbands were all the rage in the 90s, and it was not uncommon to see people of all ages sporting them on a daily basis. While they were originally designed to keep hair out of the face, they quickly became a fashion statement. Headbands came in all shapes and sizes, and there was sure to be one to suit every outfit. There was no shortage of choices, from simple black bands to glittery jewel-encrusted ones. And if you didn't like the selection on offer, you could always make your own. DIY headbands were popular, and many people took pride in their unique creations. Whether you loved them or hated them, there's no denying that headbands were a big part of the 90s.

**Combat Boots**

Whether you were rocking Doc Martens or Timberlands, these chunky boots made a bold fashion statement. They were often paired with grungy flannel shirts and ripped jeans, creating an edgy and stylish look. But combat boots weren't just for fashionistas; they were also practical. The thick soles provided ample support for walking and hiking, and the rugged construction made them ideal for outdoor activities. In the 1990s, combat boots were the footwear of choice for both style-savvy teens and adventurous adults.

**Bucket Hats**

In the 1990s, bucket hats were all the rage. Celebrities like Justin Timberlake and Britney Spears popularized the style, and soon everyone from preteens to grandparents was rocking a bucket hat. The hats became so popular that they spawned their own merchandise line, including keychains, T-shirts, and coffee mugs. Of course, like all trends, the bucket hat eventually fell out of fashion. But in recent years, it has experienced a resurgence in popularity, thanks in part to celebrities like Rihanna and Jay-Z. Whether you love them or hate them, there's no denying that bucket hats are here to stay.

**Tracksuits**

During this decade of self-expression, and fashion was one of the most popular modes of expression. Among the most iconic fashion trends of the 1990s was the tracksuit. Tracksuits became popular in hip-hop in the early 1990s and quickly spread to mainstream culture. The tracksuit was comfortable, stylish, and versatile, making it perfect for any occasion. Whether you were hitting the gym or just hanging out with friends, a tracksuit was always a good option. The tracksuit trend peaked in the mid-1990s, but it has continued to be popular in recent years as a retro style. From athleisure to streetwear, the tracksuit is an essential part of 1990s fashion.

**Baggy Jeans**

The 90s were a time of big hair, bright colors, and baggy jeans. Men and women rocked oversized denim, often with a flannel shirt or jacket tied around the waist. The trend was popularized by celebrities like Kurt Cobain and Drew Barrymore, and it soon became the go-to style for young people across the country. Even today, baggy jeans remain a popular fashion choice for many people. They are comfortable, stylish and can be dressed up or down to suit any occasion. So whether you're headed to class or going out for a night on the town, don't be afraid to rock a pair of baggy jeans – they're sure to make you look cool.

## Mom Jeans

In the 1990s, a new style of jeans emerged that would come to be known as "mom jeans." These jeans were characterized by a high waist, relaxed fit, and straight leg. They were often made from denim that was heavily faded or distressed. Mom jeans quickly became a fashion staple, appearing in magazines and on celebrities. Despite their popularity, mom jeans were often considered frumpy or unfashionable. In recent years, however, there has been a resurgence of interest in mom jeans. Many fashionistas have embraced the style as being comfortable and chic. Whether wearing them with a T-shirt and sneakers or dressing them up with a blazer and heels, mom jeans can be a versatile addition to any wardrobe.

## Flannel Shirts

In the 1990s, flannel shirts became a fashion staple for both men and women. Although the grunge look was still popular, flannel shirts were often worn as part of a more polished outfit. For example, women might pair a flannel shirt with a denim skirt or black jeans, while men might wear one with chinos or dress pants. The key to pulling off this look was to choose a shirt that fit well and to avoid looking too sloppy. In other words, it was essential to strike the right balance between casual and dressy. Although the 1990s are now considered a retro era, flannel shirts have made a comeback in recent years. Thanks to their versatility and comfort, they're once again a wardrobe essential for both men and women.

## Velour Fabric

The 90s were a great time for fashion. And one of the most popular fabrics of the decade was velour. Whether you were wearing a velour tracksuit or a velour dress, this fabric was everywhere. And it wasn't just apparel. You could also find velour on accessories like handbags and shoes. Even home furnishings like blankets and pillows were made of velour. Why was velour so popular in the 90s? Maybe it was because it was so comfortable. Or maybe it was because it had a luxurious look and feel. Whatever the reason, velour was one of the most iconic fabrics of the 90s.

**Mood Rings**

Do you remember mood rings? They were a hot item in the 90s. You would put on the ring and it would change color, supposedly based on your mood. Of course, they were really just reacting to your body temperature. But that didn't stop people from wearing them and believing in their mood-sensing powers. Even though they were mostly a gimmick, mood rings were still a lot of fun. And who knows? Maybe they did give some insight into people's emotions. After all, body temperature can be affected by stress, excitement, and other factors. In any case, mood rings were definitely a unique fashion statement of the 90s.

## Slap Bracelets

Anyone who was a child in the 1990s will remember slap bracelets. These colorful accessories were made of a metal strip covered in fabric, and they could be "slapped" onto the wrist, causing them to curl around and stay in place. Slap bracelets were trendy, and they were often given away as party favors or prizes. However, they also became the subject of safety concerns as reports surfaced of children getting injured by the metal strips. As a result, many schools banned slap bracelets, and they eventually fell out of fashion. Nevertheless, they remain a nostalgic reminder of a simpler time.

# 10

# Technology & Innovation

T hey don't make 'em like they used to. At least, that's what
we say about everything from toasters to cars to, apparently,
technology. In a recent article, Forbes made the claim that the

1990s were the last great decade for tech innovation. And you know what? They might be right.

The 1990s were a time of incredible innovation in the field of technology. The personal computer was revolutionized by introducing powerful new CPUs and GPUs, and the internet went from being a novelty to a necessity for many people.

Although the personal computer was invented in the 1970s, it wasn't until the 1990s that they really started to catch on with consumers. In 1991, only 18% of American households had a PC; by 2000, that number had jumped to 51%. A big part of this increase can be attributed to falling prices and Microsoft Windows.

Let's take a look back at some of the innovations in the 90s, the first text message was sent in 1992, and the World Wide Web was being introduced to home PCs in 1993. In 1995, the first online auction site (eBay) was launched, and Craiglist was launched in 1995 as well.

Google was founded in 1998, and 1999 saw Napster and the 32-bit Playstation console launch. It's safe to say that the 1990s were a transformative decade for the world of technology. Thanks to the inventions of the 90s, we now enjoy a level of connectedness and convenience that would have been unthinkable just a few years earlier.

One of the main reasons why we saw so much tech innovation during this decade was because it was a time of economic growth. After coming out of recession in the early '90s, businesses had more money to invest in research and development. This led to an increase in funding for tech startups, which in turn led to more innovation. We also saw an influx of talented engineers and entrepreneurs from around the world who were eager to make their mark on the burgeoning tech scene.

Overall it was a significant decade for technological innovation. The emergence of the internet, the decline in personal computer prices, and the invention of 3D console gaming all helped shape our modern world.

## The Internet in The '90s

The internet has come a long way since the 1990s. In the early days, the World Wide Web was slow, sluggish and not nearly as user-friendly as it is today. For example, there were no websites like Google or Facebook. Instead, we used sites like Yahoo and Ask Jeeves. And don't even get me started on Netscape Navigator!

Those early search engines like Yahoo! and Excite didn't have nearly as many options as Google does today. They couldn't crawl websites as effectively so their search results weren't as accurate either. As a result, finding what you were looking for on the internet could be quite challenging unless you knew exactly where to look.

We've come a long way since then, but we must remember where we came from. So let's take a trip down memory lane and explore how the internet has changed since the 1990s.

One of the biggest challenges in those early days was that internet connections were incredibly slow. Most people were using dial-up modems, which had a maximum speed of 56kbps. To put that into perspective, a typical MP3 file today is around 3mbps!

It would take hours to download a single song and even longer to load a website. Remember waiting for pictures to load on a website? That's because most images back then were around 10kb in size whereas nowadays they're usually about 1MB. Videos were practically non-existent because they would take hours to load!

Most websites in those days were very simple because they were coded in HTML (HyperText Markup Language). This language is designed to display text and images on a web page but doesn't allow for much else. As a result, most websites consisted of nothing more than a few pages of text and some images. They certainly weren't anywhere near as interactive or user-friendly as websites are today!

But internet technologies already started evolving during this decade. In the late 1990s, everyone was using Macromedia Flash to make website animations. It was the height of coolness! You could make all kinds of animated graphics and even create your own little games. Oh, how times have changed. Today, Flash is all but forgotten.

Macromedia Flash was released in 1996 and quickly became one of the most popular web design tools of the late 1990s. It allowed designers to create vector-based animations that could be played directly in a web browser. Flash was particularly popular for creating "splash pages" - those opening pages with an animation that you had to wait for before you could enter the rest of the website. Remember those?

Flash was also used to create whole website designs. Remember GeoCities? Back in the day, it was THE place to build a website. And many of those websites were built using Flash. Of course, looking back at them now, they look pretty dated and clunky. But at the time, they were cutting-edge!

It's hard to believe how far the internet has come in such a short time. What started out as a small network of computers has become a global phenomenon with billions of users worldwide. It's fantastic to think about all the things we can do online now that were completely unimaginable back in the '90s. Here's hoping that future decades bring even more fascinating advances!

# 11

# Innovative Electronics

The 90s were a golden age for electronic devices. Cell phones were slowly becoming more common, and the first Palm Pilots hit store shelves in 1996. The Sony Playstation was released in 1994, and the Nintendo 64 came out two years later. In 1998, Google was founded, and the first camera phones were introduced the following year. The 90s were also a time of great innovations in computer technology. In 1991, the first website went online, and the first web browser, Mosaic, was released in 1993. Microsoft Office was first released in 1995, and Apple's iMac debuted in 1998. The 90s were a time of great change for the electronics world, and we still feel the effects of those changes today.

**Pagers / Beepers**

If you were born in the '80s or early '90s, then you probably remember using a pager. For those of us who are old enough to remember, pagers were once a coveted accessory. In fact, they were so popular that wearing one was a status symbol.

Pagers were first introduced in the 1950s as a way for hospitals to contact doctors in the event of an emergency. But it wasn't until the 1990s that pagers became mainstream. At the time, cell phones were large, bulky, and too expensive for most people to afford. So, pagers became a popular alternative because they were small, lightweight, and relatively affordable.

Pagers also enjoyed a brief moment of popularity as a status symbol. In the 1990s, carrying a pager was a sign that you were important and busy. After all, only people with important jobs needed to be accessible at all times, right? Of course, this notion was quickly debunked when everyone, from drug dealers to teenagers, started carrying pagers. But for a brief moment in time, pagers represented power and success.

While pagers may seem like ancient history now, there was once a time when they were all the rage. Thanks to their small size, affordability, and lack of monthly service fees, pagers became a popular alternative to cell phones in the 1990s.

## Cell Phones

Can you even remember back to a time when cell phones were only used by the wealthy or business people? Well, that was once a reality. But in the 1990s, cell phone usage exploded, thanks to a series of innovations that made the devices more affordable and user-friendly. One of the most important breakthroughs was the development of digital cellular technology, which allowed for more efficient use of the radio spectrum and made it possible to connect more callers with fewer transmitter towers.

This helped to drive down the cost of cell phone service, making it more accessible to average consumers. Another key innovation was the introduction of prepaid calling plans, which gave consumers more flexibility in how they paid for their service. And finally, the launch of the first generation of so-called "smartphones" in the late 1990s paved the way for the widespread use of cell phones as personal digital assistants. Thanks to these and other innovations, cell phones went from being a luxury item to a near-essential part of daily life.

In 1992, the Nokia 1011 was released, becoming the first mass-produced GSM phone. This was followed by the launch of the world's first text messaging service in 1993. Then, in 1996, Nokia released the 2100, which was the first cell phone to include a built-in antenna. The late 90s saw even more innovative cell phones, including the release of the Palm Pilot in 1996 and the first Blackberry in 1999. These groundbreaking devices paved the way for the smartphone revolution of the 2000s.

Let's not forget about our flip phone phase. In the 1990s, flip phones were all the rage. They were sleek, stylish, and—most importantly—they allowed users to keep their privacy. With a flip phone, there was no need to worry about someone accidentally reading your text messages or listening in on your phone calls.

Instead, you could simply close the lid and know that your conversations were safe from prying eyes. Of course, flip phones also had their downside. They were notoriously difficult to use with one hand, and their small screens made it hard to stay connected to the outside world.

But for many people, the benefits of a flip phone outweighed the drawbacks. After all, there was nothing quite like the feeling of flipping open your phone and knowing that you had complete control over who could see or hear you.

## The Walkman and Portable CD Players

The '90s were a golden age for portable music players. No longer tethered to our stereos, we could finally take our tunes with us wherever we went. But there were two main types of portable music players in the '90s: the Walkman and the portable CD player.

In the late '70s, Sony released the Walkman, revolutionizing how people listen to music. Before the Walkman, music was something that was enjoyed collectively. But with the Walkman, people could suddenly listen to music anywhere they wanted, whether it was on the bus or at the beach. It gave people a new level of freedom when it came to listening to music.

In the early 90s, portable CD players began to gain popularity. These devices allowed people to listen to music with much higher fidelity than with cassette tapes. CDs also had the advantage of being much more durable than cassettes, meaning that you didn't have to worry about your favorite album getting ruined if it got dropped or wet. By the mid-'90s, portable CD players had become the rage.

One of the most significant differences between Walkmans and portable CD players was battery life. Since CDs are digital files, they don't need nearly as much power to run as cassette tapes. As a result, portable CD players often had much better battery life than Walkmans. This was a big selling point for portable CD players, especially since batteries were still relatively expensive.

The Walkman and portable CD player changed how we listen to music by giving us freedom and portability. With these devices, we can take our music with us wherever we go and listen to it on our own terms. And by being able to cherry-pick our favorite tracks, these devices have also changed how we consume music overall. Thank you, Sony and Philips, for changing how we experience music!

## Portable DVD Players

Similarly to the demand for portable CD players, portable DVD players allowed people to watch their favorite movies and TV shows on the go, and they quickly became must-have items for long car trips and plane rides. But what made them so famous? One factor was that DVDs were a relatively new technology then, and people were eager to find new ways to watch them. Portable DVD players also offered better picture quality than VHS tapes, which was another big selling point. Plus, they were becoming increasingly affordable as prices came down. As a result, portable DVD players became one of the hottest gadgets of the decade.

## The Original iMac

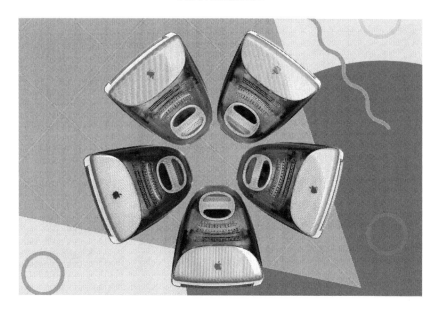

In the late 1990s, Apple was in a tough spot. The company had been struggling financially for years and was on the verge of bankruptcy. Its flagship product, the Macintosh computer, was losing market share to Microsoft's Windows operating system. However, all of that changed with the release of the iMac in 1998.

The original iMac was an all-in-one computer that combined the monitor and CPU into a single unit. It was available in a range of bright, vibrant colors that helped it stand out from the beige boxes that dominated the market at the time. It was sleek, and colorful, and came in Bondi Blue, Tangerine, Strawberry, Blueberry, Lime, Grape, Sage, Graphite, and Snow.

But it wasn't just the iMac's looks that made it popular; it was also its ease of use. The iMac ran on Apple's newly developed OS X operating system, which was much simpler to use than Windows. For many people, the iMac was their first computer experience, leaving a lasting impression.

In addition to being easy to use, the iMac was also affordable. At a time when most computers cost around $1,000, the iMac started at just $1,299. That made it a much more attractive option for families and small businesses looking to get their first computer. Not to mention, the colorful design meant that the iMac appealed to children as well as adults.

The iMac was one of the most popular computers of the 1990s, thanks to its bright colors, ease of use, and affordability. It helped Apple overcome its financial struggles and establish itself as a major player in the tech industry. These days, you can find iMacs in homes and businesses worldwide.

## Tamagotchis

The Tamagotchi was created in 1996 by the Japanese toy company Bandai. The word "Tamagotchi" is a combination of the Japanese words for "egg" and "watch." The original Tamagotchi was a simple device with few features. It had an LCD screen that showed a graphical representation of the pet and buttons that could be used to feed, clean up after, or play with the pet. As time went on and technology improved, newer versions of the Tamagotchi added more features, such as the ability to connect two devices together so that the pets could interact or compete with each other.

The appeal of the Tamagotchi was two-fold. First, they were affordable; they could be purchased for around $15-$20. Second, they were portable; they could be taken anywhere and cared for anytime. This made them especially popular with children, who could take them to school or on vacation without worrying about feeding or cleaning up after them. And unlike a real pet, if a child got tired of their Tamagotchi, they could simply turn it off and forget about it. No muss, no fuss.

By 1998, 40 million Tamagotchis had been sold worldwide, making it one of the most popular toys of all time. Today, there are dozens of virtual pet devices on the market, but none have captured the public's imagination in the same way as those original Tamagotchis did.

It's been forever now since the Tamagotchi first hit store shelves, but these little virtual pets are still fondly remembered by those who grew up in the 1990s. Simple yet addictive, the Tamagotchi became a cultural phenomenon thanks to its affordability and portability. Love them or hate them, there is no denying that these little gadgets left a big impression on those who grew up with them.

On a side note, I probably had about eight different virtual pets between

Tamagotchis, Nano babies, and Gigapets.

## Disposable Cameras

If you were a kid in the 1990s, chances are you remember disposable cameras. They were everywhere! And they were so popular that even now, 30-plus years later, people still talk about them fondly.

For many people, disposable cameras hold a special place in their hearts because they remind them of a simpler time. Before digital cameras and smartphones, taking pictures was a lot more "special." People didn't just pull out their cameras and snap a picture whenever they felt like it; they had to think about it first. That's not to say that people didn't take plenty of pictures back then—they did! It's just that with disposable cameras, every picture felt like it mattered a little bit more.

Another reason disposable cameras were so popular is that they were just so darn convenient. You didn't have to worry about re-winding the film or taking the camera back to get developed; you could just drop it off at your local drugstore and pick up your prints a few days later. Plus, if you didn't like the way your pictures turned out, oh well! You could always just buy another one.

Last but not least, disposable cameras were affordable—even for kids! If you wanted to take pictures but didn't want to spend a lot of money, all you had to do was buy a disposable camera. And if you ran out of film or dropped the camera and broke it, no big deal. You could just buy another one. Can't say the same for those fancy digital cameras nowadays.

12

# Gaming Systems

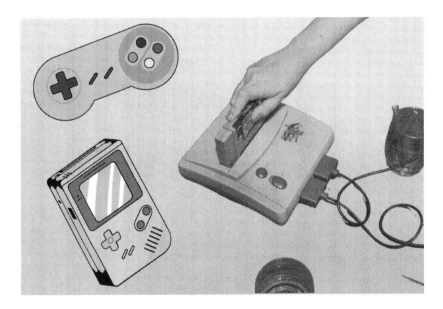

A nyone who grew up in the '90s remembers spending hours upon hours glued to a screen, whether it was playing the latest console game or desktop PC game. But what made those games so captivating?

In the early '90s, console games were all the rage. The first console game system, Nintendo's NES, was released in 1985, but it wasn't until the early 90s that console gaming started to take off. By 1993, there were three major consoles on the market: Nintendo's Super NES, Sega's Genesis, and NEC's TurboGrafx-16. These 16-bit consoles ushered in a new era of gaming with improved graphics and sound quality. Nintendo's Mario series and Sega's Sonic the Hedgehog series were particularly popular during this time.

While console games were growing in popularity, PC games were also becoming more popular thanks to advances in computer technology. IBM released its first PC in 1981, but it wasn't until the late '80s and early '90s that PCs became powerful enough to run sophisticated games. Many popular console games of the time, like Super Mario Bros. and Sonic The Hedgehog, were ported to PCs. In addition, classic PC franchises like Myst and Doom were born in the '90s.

**GameBoy - 1989**

Ah, the Gameboy is one of my favorite classics. That chunky little console that we all loved so dearly in the '90s. If you were born in a certain time period, chances are good that you spent many a childhood car ride huddled over a Gameboy, squinting at the small screen as you tried to beat your favorite game. But what was it about the Gameboy that made it so special?

It was the first portable popular gaming system. This was probably the biggest selling point of the Gameboy—the fact that you could take it with you wherever you went. Parents happily bought these for their kids as they were great for keeping kids busy on road trips. Whether you were on a long car ride or sitting in the doctor's office waiting room, the Gameboy provided entertainment on the go. Even better? The games themselves were relatively inexpensive, so you didn't have to spend a lot of money to get hours of entertainment. You may recall some of the originals like "Tetris" and "Kirby's Dreamland."

By the mid-1990s, Nintendo was facing increasing competition from other companies looking to cash in on the handheld gaming craze. Sega's Game Gear and Atari's Lynx were among the most formidable challengers, but neither could match Nintendo's dominance. In 1996, Nintendo released an updated version of the Gameboy, dubbed the "Gameboy Pocket," which was smaller, lighter, and more power-efficient than its predecessor.

Then in 1998 the Gameboy Color was released. It was a 32-bit handheld system that was backward compatible with all of the original Gameboy's cartridges. It featured a color screen (hence the name) as well as improved sound quality. In addition to all of the games that could be played on the original Gameboy, there were also several titles that were exclusive to the Color version. These include The Legend of Zelda: Oracle of Ages and Pokémon Gold and Silver.

One of the most popular Gameboy games of the 90s was Tetris. This puzzle game captivated gamers with its simple yet addictive gameplay. Another popular choice was Super Mario Land, which allowed players to explore new worlds like everyone's favorite plumber. Lastly, Pokémon Red and Blue were two of the most popular games of the decade, introducing a generation of kids to the world of pocket monsters.

Why did we love our Gameboys so much back in the day? Nostalgia surely plays a role, but there's no denying that those little gray consoles packed a serious punch in terms of entertainment value. From their portability to their ease of use to their timeless appeal, there's a lot to love about those classic Gameboys—and we're sure anyone who owned one back in the '90s would agree!

## Sega Genesis - 1988

It's been over thirty years since the heyday of the 16-bit gaming console wars when Nintendo and Sega went head to head in living rooms across America. These days, Nintendo is still king in console gaming, but there's been a recent resurgence in interest in Sega's classic console, the Sega Genesis.

The Genesis boasted superior graphics and processing power compared to its 8-bit NES rival—but more importantly, it had better games. At launch, the Genesis came bundled with versions of arcade hits like "Altered Beast" and "Golden Axe." In 1991, Sega released "Sonic the Hedgehog," quickly becoming one of the most popular games ever. Thanks to its excellent library of games—not to mention some canny marketing by Sega—the Genesis quickly gained ground on Nintendo's

NES in North America. By 1993, Sega had secured 35% of the 16-bit market share in North America.

The war between Nintendo and Sega reached its zenith when Nintendo released its Super Nintendo Entertainment System (SNES) console. Although it was technically inferior to the Genesis, the SNES had better graphics and an excellent lineup of first-party games that kept gamers coming back for more. As a result, Nintendo once again regained control of the home console market. In 1997, Sega finally conceded defeat and discontinued production of all 16-bit hardware.

**Super Nintendo - 1990**

The Super Nintendo holds a special place in the hearts of many millennials. It was the console that defined our childhoods, after all. From classics like Super Mario World and Donkey Kong Country to newer favorites like Super Mario and Kirby's Dream Course, there was simply nothing else like it. But what made the Super Nintendo so special?

While the original Nintendo console was groundbreaking in its day, the Super Nintendo was truly in a class of its own. Released in 1990, the Super Nintendo featured 16-bit graphics that were significantly more advanced than anything that had come before. In addition, the Super Nintendo featured a wide variety of games that appealed to gamers of all ages. From classic titles like "Super Mario World" and "Legend of Zelda: A Link to the Past" to more mature offerings like "Final Fantasy IV" and "Chrono Trigger," Super Nintendo had something for everyone. In addition, the SuperNintendo also featured groundbreaking Mode 7 graphics that allowed for some truly impressive visuals. All of these factors combined to make the Super Nintendo one of the most popular consoles ever released.

In many ways, the release of the Super Nintendo signaled a bright future for video gaming. With better hardware came better graphics and sound, which allowed developers to create more immersive and exciting worlds for players to explore. Combined with an excellent lineup of launch titles and strong support from third-party developers, it's no wonder that so many gamers fell in love with their SNES consoles. While we may never see another console quite like it, the legacy of the Super Nintendo will live on forever in the hearts of those who experienced its magic firsthand.

**Sega Game Gear - 1990**

The handheld console from Sega was touted as a superior alternative to Nintendo's device, with better graphics and more games. But why was the Game Gear so popular?

The answer may have something to do with marketing. In the early 1990s, Nintendo was still enjoying enormous success with the original Game Boy, which was released in 1989. Sega saw an opportunity to grab a piece of the market share and introduced the Game Gear in 1991. The company rolled out a big marketing campaign that featured celebrities like Michael Jordon and Mike Tyson (who had his own game for the console). It also positioned the device as a "grown-up" alternative to Nintendo's console, which was seen as more juvenile.

Whatever the reason, kids flocked to stores to get their hands on a Game Gear. And there were plenty of games to choose from—Sega had already ported over many of its popular titles from its Master System console, including "Sonic the Hedgehog," "Alex Kidd," and "Golden Axe." The company also secured licenses for popular franchises like "Batman" and "Star Wars." And for kids who wanted something different from what Nintendo was offering, there were plenty of original games available for the Game Gear as well.

When the Game Gear first launched in 1991, its graphics were down-right impressive. The console was capable of displaying a palette of 32,768 colors, which was unheard of at the time. This allowed for some seriously colorful games that looked great on the vehicle-sized screen. Not to mention, the graphics were miles ahead of anything that could be found on rival handheld consoles like the Nintendo Game Boy. Personally, hands down, the Sega Game Gear was my favorite. My only complaint about this gaming system was the battery life.

The Sega Game Gear was one of our favorite handheld gaming consoles growing up in the '90s, and there are a few reasons why it was so popular back then. From its impressive graphics to its wide selection of great games, there was a lot to love about this hand held console.

**Playstation - 1994**

The original PlayStation console was released in 1994 and was an instant hit. Sony's cutting-edge gaming system quickly rose to prominence, becoming the MUST-HAVE gaming console of the '90s. But how did PlayStation become so popular?

The release of the original PlayStation console in 1994 was a turning point for the gaming industry. Prior to the PlayStation, most video game consoles were limited to cartridges that could only hold a small amount of data. The PlayStation, on the other hand, used CDs, which could hold much more data. This allowed developers to create richer and more immersive gaming experiences than ever before. And gamers loved it!

In addition to its cutting-edge hardware, the PlayStation also had an impressive lineup of launch titles that included classics like Ridge Racer, Final Fantasy VII, Crash Bandicoot, and Tekken. These games showed off the power of the PlayStation and helped convince early adopters that this was a console worth investing in.

Of course, no discussion of the rise of the PlayStation would be complete without mention of Sony's aggressive marketing campaign. Sony pulled out all the stops from TV ads featuring popular celebrities to edgy print ads to get people talking about their new console. And it worked! Thanks in part to Sony's stellar marketing efforts, the PlayStation quickly became THE must-have gaming console of the '90s.

**Nintendo 64 - 1996**

Nintendo released the Nintendo 64 in 1996, and it quickly became one of the most popular game consoles of the 1990s. There are a number of reasons why the console was so popular, from its innovative hardware to its diverse library of games.

One of the most important factors in the popularity of the Nintendo 64 was its innovative hardware. The console was one of the first to feature 3D graphics, and its 64-bit processor allowed for significantly more detailed graphics than previous consoles. In addition, the Nintendo 64 featured four controller ports, which allowed up to four people to play together at once—a feature that was unique at the time and helped make party games like Mario Party and Super Smash Bros. hugely popular.

In addition to its innovative hardware, the Nintendo 64 had a great selection of games. While other consoles only had a few must-play titles, the Nintendo 64 had dozens of top-notch games, including classics like Super Mario 64, The Legend of Zelda: Ocarina of Time, Mario Kart 64, and GoldenEye 007. There was something for everyone on the Nintendo 64, from party games and platformers to first-person shooters and role-playing games. And thanks to its powerful hardware, the Nintendo 648 could handle 3D games with ease—something that other consoles couldn't do at the time.

The Nintendo 64 was one of the most popular game consoles of the 1990s, thanks to its innovative hardware and diverse selection of games. Even though it's been over 20 years since its release, many fans still fondly remember playing their favorite N64 games.

# 13

# Conclusion

What's Not to Love About the '90s?!
It's hard to believe that the '90s are now considered a
"nostalgia decade." After all, it doesn't seem like that long
ago that we were living in the moment and enjoying everything the '90s
had to offer. But time flies and the '90s are now looked back on fondly
as a simpler time. Let's recap on what made the '90s such a special time.

## The Music

The '90s were a golden age for music, with new genres and subgenres
emerging almost every year. There was something for everyone from
grunge and garage rock to boy bands and girl power pop. The decade
also saw the rise of hip-hop and R&B, which would go on to dominate
the charts in the 2000s. But despite all of these different genres and
subgenres, one thing was for sure: the music of the '90s was just plain
fun. Whether you were jamming out to Nirvana or TLC, committing
every word of "Snow" by Porno for Pyros to memory or dancing your
heart out to "Baby One More Time," there was no shortage of great

tunes to enjoy in the '90s.

## The Movies

The '90s were also a great decade for movies. In addition to classics like Forrest Gump, The Shawshank Redemption, and Pulp Fiction, we also got our first taste of big blockbuster franchises like Jurassic Park, The Matrix, and Toy Story. And let's not forget about animated films like Aladdin, Mulan, and The Lion King, which introduced a whole new generation of kids to the magic of Disney. Whether you were looking for a laugh-out-loud comedy or a heart-wrenching drama, there was definitely a '90s movie for you.

## The Technology

It's hard to believe that the first mobile phones were introduced in the '80s! But it wasn't until the '90s that they really started to catch on. By 1998, 50 million people worldwide were using them—and that number would only continue to grow in the years that followed. Of course, mobile phones weren't the only new technology of the '90s. The World Wide Web also emerged as a major force during this decade, giving rise to new companies like Google and Amazon. And let's not forget about those iconic gadgets like Tamagotchis and Walkmans!

Overall, there's no denying that the '90s were a special decade—but what made them so special? Was it the music? The movies? The technology? Or was it something else entirely? I think it might just be that sense of nostalgia we feel when we look back on those ten years… after all, they really were simpler times. Thanks for taking a trip down memory lane with me! I hope you enjoyed it as much as I did.

If you enjoyed throwing it back to the good ole' days or this book simply made you smile I would appreciate if you could drop it a review. Feel free to leave a comment in your review and let us know some of your favorite things from the '90s.

# 14

# References

Barrett, J. (2021, August 28). *15 Things That Happened In The '90s That We'll Never Forget*. Redbook. Retrieved 13 October 2022, from https://www.redbookmag.com/life/charity/g3108804 1/memorable-90s-events/

Hossain, J. (2022, July 15). *Top 100 Artists Of The 90s*. Top40Weekly.com. Retrieved 13 October 2022, from https://top40weekly.com/top-100-artists-of-the-90s/

Jaime, & Purvis. (2016, July 5). *9 Tech Products You Had in the '90s*. The List TV. Retrieved 13 October 2022, from https://www.thelisttv.com/the-list/9-tech-products-you-had-in-the-90s/

Shabazz, S. (2020, August 19). *20 Reasons Why The '90s Were The Best Decade To Grow Up In*. Scary Mommy. Retrieved 13 October 2022, from https://www.scarymommy.com/90s-were-best-decade-grow-up

Stieg, C. (2016, October 1). *18 Gadgets You Forgot You Were Totally Obsessed With in the '90s and '00s*. Good Housekeeping. Retrieved 13

October 2022, from https://www.goodhousekeeping.com/life/entertainment/advice/g3893/gadgets-you-were-obsessed-with-90s/